D1277130

to...

with love...

date...

God Loves His Precious Children

Jim & Elizabeth George

Paintings by Judy Luenebrink

HARVEST HOUSE PUBLISHERS

EUGENE, OREGON

God Loves His Precious Children

Text copyright © 2004 by Jim and Elizabeth George

Illustrations copyright © 2004 by Judy Luenebrink

Published by Harvest House Publishers

Eugene, Oregon 97402

Library of Congress Cataloging-in-Publication Data
George, Jim, 1943-
    God loves his precious children / Jim and Elizabeth George ; illustrations by Judy Luenebrink.
    p. cm.
    ISBN 0-7369-1137-5
    1. Children—Religious life—Juvenile literature.   I. George, Elizabeth, 1944- II. Luenebrink, Judy.   III. Title.
    BV4571.3.G46 2004
    242'.62—dc22
    2004001052

Design and production by Matthew Shoemaker

Scripture quotations are from *The International Children's Bible*, New Century Version,
copyright © 1986 by Word Publishing, Nashville, Tennessee. Used by permission.

All rights reserved. No part of this publication may be reproduced, stored in a retrieval system,
or transmitted in any form or by any means—electronic, mechanical, digital, photocopy, recording,
or any other—except for brief quotations in printed reviews, without the prior permission of the publisher.

Printed in China.

04 05 06 07 08 09 10 11 12 13 / IM / 10 9 8 7 6 5 4 3 2 1

For more information regarding the authors and illustrator of this book, please contact:

Jim & Elizabeth George
Jim & Elizabeth George Ministries
P.O. Box 2879
Belfair, WA 98528
1-800-542-4611
www.jimgeorge.com
www.elizabethgeorge.com

Judy Luenebrink
7057 Hatillo Avenue
Winnetka, CA 91306
1-818-888-9934

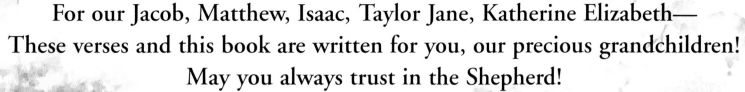

For our Jacob, Matthew, Isaac, Taylor Jane, Katherine Elizabeth—
These verses and this book are written for you, our precious grandchildren!
May you always trust in the Shepherd!

Dear Friend,

Psalm 23 has been called "The Shepherd Psalm." Perhaps that's because it is such a beautiful and timeless picture of the Shepherd's care for His people and the "sheep" of His pasture (Psalm 100:3).

And who better to become acquainted—at an early age—with the character of God than His precious children? Indeed, a strong knowledge of our all-knowing and ever-present God will support a child through all the days of his or her life.

It is our prayer that these heartwarming rhymes, based on this cherished psalm, will bless the children in your life and increase their understanding of God. May this book and the delightful art of Judy Luenebrink encourage them to grow in faith and to rest in God's love.

Come journey along with your precious ones! Allow these truths to again refresh and encourage your faith in God's character and His care for you, too!

In His love,

Jim and Elizabeth

Growing up's a journey each child loves to take—
A trek filled with roads, both crooked and straight,
Paths in the shade, and some bright cheery sun,
And days of adventure…packed full of fun!

"What all should I take?" Oh, don't bother 'bout that!
God knows what you'll need…plus He's got the map!
Through all the excitement, 'til your travels are done,
The Lord will be with you…you're His precious one!

Every child needs someone, a person who cares,
God is that Someone, the Bible declares.
I don't have to worry, I need never fear;
The Lord is my Shepherd—He's always right here!

"The Lord is my Shepherd."
PSALM 23:1A

Because the Lord takes care of me,
I have everything I need.
A cozy place, a bed for sleep,
A loving Friend...and lots to eat!

❧

"I have everything I need."
PSALM 23:1B

I love being busy, to run and to play,
In fact, I believe I could romp all day!
But God always knows exactly what's best—
He knows there are times I just need to rest.

"He gives me rest in green pastures."
PSALM 23:2A

"I'm tired! I'm thirsty! I'm falling apart!"
These are the cries of an unhappy heart.
But then I recall, "God's right by my side,
To comfort and calm, to cheer and to guide."

"He leads me to calm water."
PSALM 23:2B

Do you ever just need a good pat on the back,
Especially when things seem to dim and turn black?
A touch from the Shepherd can make things so bright,
When He says, "Be strong in the strength of My might!"

"He gives me new strength."
PSALM 23:3A

How can a kid know which way is best,
When two paths appear and offer a test?
The answer is clear—when two choices arise,
Choose *God's* way! That's doing what's wise.

*"For the good of his name,
he leads me on paths that are right."*
PSALM 23:3B

Because they don't know the Shepherd by heart,
A few of my friends are scared of the dark!
But no matter how frightful the shadows may be,
I'll not be afraid—my Shepherd's with me.

*"Even if I walk through a very dark valley,
I will not be afraid because you are with me."*
PSALM 23:4A

When I hear a strange noise, I imagine the worst.
My heart flips and flutters 'til I think it might burst!
But then I remember God's promise to me—
"Fear not, precious one, *I'm* walking with thee."

*"Your rod and your walking
stick comfort me."*
PSALM 23:4B

Do you have a good friend who cares about you?
Someone who's loyal, who's faithful and true?
God's your "best friend" and your greatest treasure.
He shares all He has and gives beyond measure.

"You pour oil on my head.
You give me more than I can hold."
PSALM 23:5A

I'm frequently warned, "Don't talk to strangers,"
To watch where I walk and to flee life's dangers.
But in spite of the "things" that are lurking about,
God's standing on guard to protect and look out.

*"You prepare a meal for me
in front of my enemies"*
PSALM 23:5B

Isn't it great that the journey's not done?
Ahead's a whole life of adventures and fun!
And no matter how trying my days or each task,
God's goodness and love are *sure* to hold fast.

*"Surely your goodness and love
will be with me all my life."*
PSALM 23:6A

No matter what happens or where we may roam,
God's there at the end to welcome us "Home"!
And what will I find when I step through the door?
All that I need...forevermore.

*"And I will live in the house
of the Lord forever."*
PSALM 23:6B

Words to Know

The Word	What It Means
precious	of great value, very special, cherished
My might	God's power
imagine	think of
thee	another way of saying "you"
loyal	committed
faithful	can be counted on
frequency	often
lurking	hanging around
forevermore	for eternity